PAUL T. NICHOLSON

EGYPTIAN FAIENCE
AND GLASS

SHIRE EGYPTOLOGY

2

Cover illustration
A polychrome glass fish vessel from Amarna. Core-formed vessels such as this served as containers for cosmetics. Eighteenth Dynasty, reign of Akhenaten. Length 145 mm. (Courtesy of Peter Clayton. British Museum EA 55193.)

British Library Cataloguing in Publication Data
Nicholson, Paul T.
Egyptian Faience and Glass.- (Shire Egyptology Series; No.19)
I. Title II. Series 932
ISBN 0-7478-0197-5

For my parents

Published by
SHIRE PUBLICATIONS LTD
Cromwell House, Church Street, Princes Risborough,
Buckinghamshire HP27 9AJ, UK.

Series Editor: Barbara Adams.

ISBN 0 7478 0195 9.

First published 1993.

Printed in Great Britain by
CIT Printing Services, Press Buildings,
Merlins Bridge, Haverfordwest, Dyfed SA61 1XF.

Contents

Acknowledgements

I am particularly grateful to the following for their help in the production of this book: Janine Bourriau and Professor M. S. Tite for their helpful advice and for reading the text in draft, and Professor R. G. Newton for discussions on glass-making technology.

Thanks are also due to Barry Kemp and to the Committee of the Egypt Exploration Society for allowing me to use material from the Amarna excavations and to many of my colleagues from that project who have assisted me, particularly Andy Boyce in discussing some of his ideas on faience production, and Willeke Wendrich for reading an early draft of part of this book. Dr H.L. Patterson kindly provided information on majolica. Kate Trott kindly edited the final version of the text and produced the drawings.

I am indebted to many friends, colleagues and institutions for the use of illustrations and these are gratefully acknowledged in the captions. Photographs of objects in the Petrie Museum of Egyptian Archaeology are by the author.

The outline chronology is based on that of Dr William J. Murnane and acknowledgement is made to him and to Penguin Books for its use here.

4

List of illustrations

Chronology

Based on W. J. Murnane, *The Penguin Guide to Ancient Egypt*, 1983.

Predynastic and Protodynastic Period	before 3050 BC		
Early Dynastic Period	3050 - 2613 BC		
		3050-2682	Dynasties I and II
		2686-2613	Dynasty III
		2668-2649	*Djoser*
Old Kingdom	2613 - 2181 BC		
		2613-2498	Dynasty IV
		2498-2345	Dynasty V
			Raneferef
		2477-2467	*Neferirkare*
		2453-2422	*Niuserre*
		2345-2181	Dynasty VI
First Intermediate Period	2181 - 2040 BC		
		2181-2040	Dynasties VII-X
		2134-2060	Dynasty XI (Theban)
Middle Kingdom	2040 - 1782 BC		
		2060-1991	Dynasty XI
		1991-1782	Dynasty XIII
		1971-1928	*Sesostris I*
		1842-1797	*Amenemhat III*
			Nubkheperre Inyotef
Second Intermediate Period	1782 - 1570 BC		
		1782-1650	Dynasties XIII and XIV (Egyptian)
		1663-1555	Dynasties XV and XVI (Hyksos)
		1663-1570	Dynasty XVII (Theban)
New Kingdom	1570 - 1070 BC		
		1570-1293	Dynasty XVIII
		1570-1546	*Ahmose*
		1551-1524	*Amenophis I*
		1524-1518	*Tuthmosis I*
		1504-1450	*Tuthmosis III*
		1498-1483	*Hatshepsut*
		1453-1419	*Amenophis II*

	1386-1349	*Amenophis III*
	1350-1334	*Amenophis IV*
		(Akhenaten)
	1334-1325	*Tutankhamun*
	1293-1185	Dynasty XIX
	1279-1212	*Ramesses II*

Third 1070 - 713 BC
Intermediate
Period

	1070-945	Dynasty XXI
	1070-1026	*Pinedjem I (Thebes)*
	978-959	*Siamun*
	945-712	Dynasty XXII
	828-712	Dynasty XXIII
	724-713	Dynasty XXIV

Late Period 713 - 332 BC

	713-656	Dynasty XXV (Nubian)
	664-525	Dynasty XXVI
	664-610	*Psammetichus I*
	570-526	*Amasis*
	525-404	Dynasty XXVI
		(Persian)
	521-486	*Darius I*
	404-399	Dynasty XXVIII
	399-380	Dynasty XXIX
	380-343	Dynasty XXX
		(Egyptian/Persian)
	360-342	*Nectanebo II*

Graeco-Roman 332 BC - AD 395
Period

	332-30	Ptolemies
	247-222	*Ptolemy III*

30 BC - AD 395 Roman Emperors

Period	Body Manufacture	Glazing Process	Factory Evidence
Predynastic (5500-3050 BC)	Modelling a core for grinding Surface grinding Free form modelling (rare)	Application (?) Cementation (?) Efflorescence (?)	None
Proto-Early Dynastic (3200-2613 BC)	Modelling Surface grinding	Efflorescence	None
Old Kingdom (2613-2181 BC)	Painting with slurry Layering (rare)		None
First Intermediate (2181-2040 BC)	Core forming (rare) Marbleising (rare) Moulding (?)		None
Middle Kingdom (2040-1782 BC)	Modelling Moulding on a form	Efflorescence Cementation	Lisht Kerma
Second Intermediate (1782-1570 BC)	Core forming Marbleising Layering Painting with coloured quartz slurry Incising Inlaying Resisting Painting with pigment wash	Application	
New Kingdom (1570-1070 BC)	Moulding on a form Pressing into openface moulds Forming over a core Joining of moulded parts with quartz slurry Layering Incising Inlaying with quartz slurry Painting with pigment wash Throwing	Efflorescence Application Finely powdered glass added to body or inlay to extend colour range	Amarna Lisht
Later Periods (1070 BC-395 AD)	All of New Kingdom techniques plus throwing (?)	Application Efflorescence	Memphis Naucratis

Methods of Egyptian faience manufacture by period. (Courtesy of P. Vandiver.)

PART I: FAIENCE

1

The material

Introduction

Faience, more correctly termed 'Egyptian faience', has been a source of confusion almost since its rediscovery, and this confusion is still encountered today. However, in an attempt to understand the material, much valuable work has been done by archaeological scientists and this has helped in piecing together a fascinating technological history of the material to stand beside the more traditional typological approach.

The name *faience* comes from a tin-glazed earthenware, made at Faenze in northern Italy and elsewhere from the late medieval period. For a time faience was used to refer to any similar lustrous pottery, though the term has now been replaced by the more accurate *majolica*. It was the bright colours of this pottery which came to the minds of Europeans on encountering Egyptian faience. Once the origin of the name is understood, there seems little reason to seek an alternative, though confusing attempts have been made to do so.

Faience has been called 'the first high-tech ceramic' to emphasise its status as an artificial medium, effectively an artificial precious stone.

It is a non-clay ceramic composed of crushed quartz or sand with small amounts of lime and either natron or plant ash. This body is coated with a soda-lime-silica glaze which is generally a bright blue-green colour due to the use of copper. Pamela Vandiver has determined the typical body to be 92-99 per cent SiO_2 (silicon dioxide), 1-5 per cent CaO (calcium oxide), 0.5-3 per cent Na_2O (sodium oxide) with minor quantities of CuO (cuprous oxide), Al_2O_3 (aluminium oxide), TiO_2 (titanium oxide), MgO (magnesium oxide) and K_2O (potassium oxide). The forming of the body and glaze varies considerably over time, not least according to the status of the workshop, those under royal patronage apparently having better access to materials and freedom to experiment while smaller local concerns perhaps tended towards conservatism.

The typical faience mixture is thixotropic, that is, thick at first and then soft and flowing as it begins to be deformed, though it cracks if deformed too rapidly. This property makes the material

Application of glaze slurry

Thickness depends on body porosity and water content of slurry.

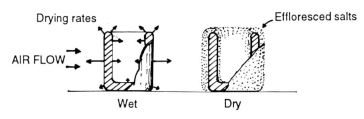

Efflorescence of glaze

Thickness depends on drying rate.

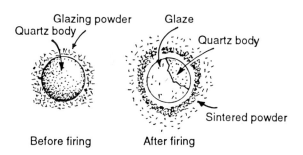

Cementation of glaze

Thickness depends on firing time and temperature.

1. Methods of faience glazing. (Courtesy of P. Vandiver, after Vandiver in Kaczmarczyk and Hedges, *Ancient Egyptian Faience*, 1983, page 145.)

more difficult to work than potting clay and so demands a different technique. Various shaping techniques were employed, which are discussed chronologically below. Once the desired form was achieved the object could be fired.

Firing temperatures for faience have been subject to debate, though most authorities now accept a range between 800 and 1000°C.

Several faience workshops are known, ranging from a possible Middle Kingdom example, through the Eighteenth Dynasty, to the Ptolemaic/Roman period, though the full technological sequence used in these is not yet clear (see the table on page 8).

The ancient Egyptians knew faience as *thenet,* a term sometimes, though rarely, applied to glass. The derivation of the word is from 'dazzling' or 'shining'; the optical effect of faience, particularly when a fine white quartz layer underlies the glaze, is that of a precious stone and it was probably intended to resemble turquoise or lapis lazuli.

Glazing methods

Faience can be glazed using several different techniques, whose frequencies of use varied over time (figure 1).

Efflorescence. This is a so-called self-glazing technique in which water-soluble alkali salts such as the carbonates, sulphates and chlorides of sodium and, less commonly, potassium, in the form of natron or plant ash are mixed with the quartz material making up the core of the artefact. Analyses suggest that from the Predynastic into Roman times there was a general preference for alkali derived from plant ashes rather than natron. During drying, these salts migrate to the surface of the object to form an effloresced crust or bloom. On firing, this layer melts and fuses with the fine quartz, copper oxide and lime. This technique can be recognised on artefacts by variations in the thickness of the glaze. For example, where the object has been in contact with a surface, or where secondary working of the shape has taken place and the surface has been cut away, efflorescence is reduced or prevented, leaving a thin glaze or no glaze at all. The glaze is thickest where drying has been greatest, thus exterior surfaces are generally better glazed than interior ones. This technique has the greatest amount of interstitial glass (the glassy phase in the interstices between quartz particles), and the interface between glaze and core is generally clearest. It was probably the technique most commonly used by the ancient Egyptians (figure 2).

Cementation. This, too, is a self-glazing technique, in which the unglazed but dry faience core is buried in a glazing powder which

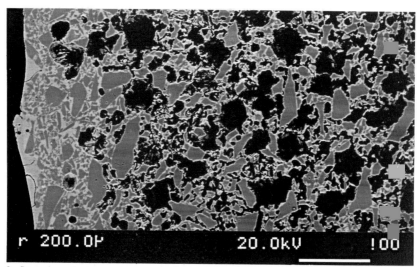

2. Scanning electron microscope photograph of section through faience glazed by efflorescence. From an Eighteenth Dynasty faience vessel from Amarna. The glaze and interstitial glass show as pale grey, quartz as darker grey and voids as black. (Courtesy of the Petrie Museum of Egyptian Archaeology, University College London, and Professor M. S. Tite. UC 30153.)

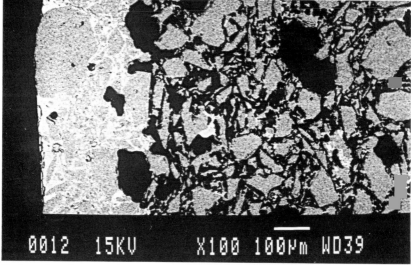

3. Scanning electron microscope photograph of section through faience glazed by cementation. From a Twenty-first Dynasty shabti. The glaze shows white, the quartz grey and the pores black. (Courtesy of the Trustees of the British Museum and Professor M. S. Tite. BMRL 16323.)

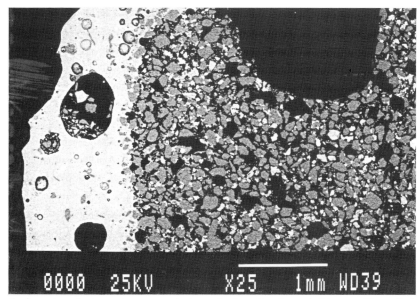

4. Scanning electron microscope photograph of section through faience with applied glaze. From a Late Period shabti. The quartz shows grey, while the glass is white and the pores show black. (Courtesy of the Trustees of the British Museum and Professor M. S. Tite. BMRL 16322.)

partially melts on heating. The powder reacts with the surface of the quartz core and so glazes it, though powder not in contact with it remains unaffected and can be crumbled away from the glazed object once firing is completed. The powder is composed of lime (that is, calcium oxide), ash, silica, charcoal and colorant, and a range of different mixtures has been found to work experimentally. The method is sometimes known as the 'Qom technique', after a village in Iran where it was first recorded, in the 1960s, by an engineer researching the traditional crafts of the area. It can be recognised by the fairly uniform all-over glaze, which is often quite thin, the absence of drying marks, and by the lack of firing marks for small objects, though there may be rough surfaces on larger pieces where they rested during firing. Occasionally the glaze may be thicker on the underside of pieces produced by this method. The interface between glaze and core is generally well defined, and there is very little interstitial glass (figure 3).

Application. It used to be assumed that this was the method used in all faience manufacture, since it was familiar to Europeans as their method of glazing ceramics. It involves the application of a glazing powder, or slurry, to the faience core. The object can be immersed in the mixture or it can be painted on. The powder part of the slurry may comprise quartz, lime and natron which have been ground up together, or raw materials which have been fritted together (see glossary) and then crushed. The open-textured quartz body absorbs some of this mixture so that it adheres to it and forms a coating on drying, though the amount of interstitial glass is not great and the interface of glaze and core is not well defined. In firing, this coating melts to leave a glaze, which is often quite thick. Only one firing is necessary, unlike the glazing of pottery where the body is sometimes first given a biscuit (bisque) firing before application of the glaze. This method is recognisable by the presence of drips, brush marks or flow lines and the greater thickness of the glaze layer. It may also have a clear edge where the application ceases in order to prevent the object sticking to kiln supports during the firing, or to enable the object to be moved more easily (figure 4).

Faience often has details added to it in black or brown slurry or paint coloured with manganese and iron oxides, which then fires hard along with the object. This becomes common from the Old Kingdom onwards. It should be noted, however, that these techniques are not always readily identifiable and that combined techniques were sometimes used.

Classification

In his treatise *Ancient Egyptian Materials and Industries*, first published in 1926, Alfred Lucas (Chemist to the Egyptian Antiquities Service) divided faience into categories based on visual criteria. Although not employed here, the categories are outlined since they are frequently found in the archaeological literature. As the categories say little about the method of manufacture and can mask technological information, a detailed description combined with a suggestion as to glazing method is preferable. Lucas's classes are:

Ordinary faience: the typical Egyptian faience consisting of a body material (core) coated with vitreous alkaline glaze.

Variant A: faience with an extra layer between core and glaze; this is usually composed of fine ground white quartz (figure 5).

Variant B: black faience, which is rare.

Variant C: red faience; the body material is usually coloured red, though the glaze may also be red, and occasionally only the glaze is coloured and the body white.

Variant D: faience with a hard blue or green body.

Variant E: glassy faience, which is not a true faience at all, but rather an imperfect form of glass, included as a frit by recent researchers and probably developed from the addition of glass and alkali to a faience body (figure 6).

Variant F: faience with a lead glaze, thought by Lucas to be a Twenty-second Dynasty introduction, though this view may be subject to revision with the discovery of some glass from Amarna containing lead.

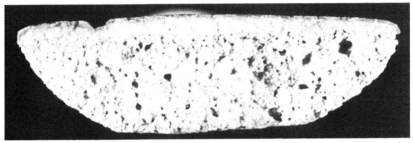

5. Section through faience inlay. A fine quartz layer underlies the glaze improving its optical properties; coarser material makes up the lower portion. The piece was glazed by efflorescence. From Amarna. Length 19 mm. (Courtesy of the Egypt Exploration Society. Photograph by Gwil Owen. Object 8340.)

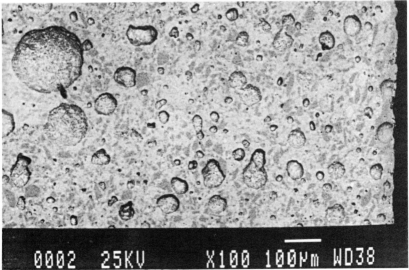

6. Scanning electron microscope photograph of section through glassy faience. From a Twenty-fifth or Twenty-sixth Dynasty shabti. Unreacted quartz shows grey, precipitated devitrite in white, the dark rings delineate air bubbles. (Courtesy of the Trustees of the British Museum and Professor M. S. Tite. EA 34095.)

Alternative terms

A number of other terms have been used as alternatives for faience. These include 'glazed composition', 'porcelain', and 'frit' or 'blue frit'. Such alternatives are best avoided since 'Egyptian faience' is well established and is quite adequate so long as it is used to refer only to this quartz-based, soda-lime-silica glazed material. Furthermore, some of these 'alternative' designations actually refer to other materials. Since these terms frequently cause confusion they are briefly defined here.

Porcelain is a particular type of white-bodied clay ceramic first produced in medieval China and imported from the fifteenth century into Europe, where it became widely imitated. It should not be used as an alternative to 'faience'.

Frit is a rather ambiguous term. It can be used to refer to the product of 'fritting' — the solid state reaction which forms the first stage in glass production (see Glass section); or to a material commonly used as a pigment or to make artefacts in its own right. Recent work has divided frits into two groups: blue frits, whose dominant crystalline phase is a copper calcium silicate known as 'Egyptian blue' in a very limited matrix of glass, and turquoise-blue frits, in which the dominant phase other than quartz is a calcium silicate known as wollastonite, which is crystallised from the copper-rich glass matrix. The frits can each be subdivided into coarse and fine textured, the coarse normally representing the first stage of production, which would then be ground finer and moulded into artefacts or used as a pigment.

Egyptian blue appears to be an Egyptian invention and, though of much greater antiquity, is closely allied to glass (figure 7). Its texture may be so fine that it is virtually indistinguishable from glass, especially if the latter is weathered. It is known by the Old Kingdom and undergoes gradual refinement, becoming increasingly glass-like, into the early Roman period. It was known to the Greeks as *kyanos*, while Vitruvius knew it as *caeruleum*, and believed it to have been invented at Alexandria.

Despite the possible confusion with glass, the frits are easily distinguished from faience (at least where a broken section can be viewed) by the lack of a core; they are homogeneous throughout and have no separate glaze layer.

Faience, frits and glass are part of a continuum of materials based on silica plus varying amounts of alkali, lime and copper, though they are distinct in terms of their composition since it would not be possible to turn faience into frit or frit into glass simply by prolonging heating or firing at a higher temperature. The addition of further

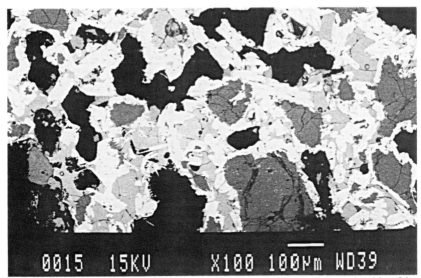

7. Scanning electron microscope photograph of section through Egyptian blue frit. From a Roman mosaic of the second century AD. Unreacted quartz appears dark grey, crystals of Egyptian blue as white and the glass matrix as light grey. (Courtesy of the Trustees of the British Museum and Professor M. S. Tite. EB 14122.)

8. One craftsman, believed by Nolte to be a faience maker, mixes ingredients (right), while another works on a completed piece (left). From the tomb of Ibi (Aba), chief steward of the divine adoratress in the time of Psammetichus I. Thebes (TT36), Twenty-sixth Dynasty. The full scene shows other craft activities. (After Davies, *The Rock Tombs of Deir el Gebrawi*, London, 1902, plate 25.)

alkali would be necessary. Nonetheless, this may give a clue to how the ancient Egyptians might have organised their 'vitreous materials' industry (figure 8). It is not unlikely that faience, frit and glass were all made in close proximity, possibly in the same workshop complex, so that developments in one may be reflected in others.

2

Predynastic

The first glazing

Glazed steatite and faience beads are known from Predynastic graves at Naqada, Badari, el-Amrah, Matmar, Harageh, Abadiyeh, el-Gerzeh and elsewhere. At these sites semi-precious stones such as turquoise and lapis lazuli are also found and, although glazed steatite is the most common, faience is definitely established. The glaze is blue or blue-green, probably in imitation of these stones and, perhaps, of green feldspar. The glazing of stones is not to be confused with the making of faience since here glaze is applied to a solid natural object rather than to an artificial body. How the transition to faience was made must remain a matter of speculation, but it is likely that, once discovered, the faience technique was to be preferred, since the irregular core surface would help to give a brighter, more sparkling appearance to the glaze than would the flat surface of steatite or quartz pebbles.

Recent analyses of material from Naqada show that the composition of the faience varies considerably even within one grave, suggesting that the copper used in the mixture came either from several sources or from one very variable source.

The faience beads seem to be hand-formed from crushed quartz, plant ashes or natron, and malachite mixed with water. This mixture is thixotropic, and so required specific working techniques. Shapes were probably roughly modelled and then abraded to the final form once dry, when holes could also be bored. The object could then be fired. The same techniques were used in figurines (figure 9).

This earliest phase in the development of faience is thought to be one of the more diverse in terms of technology, when a number of forming and glazing techniques were experimented with. Beads of this period (Naqada I and II) have an overall glaze, some showing firing marks, others not, which can be uneven. This suggests that all three main techniques of production found in later times may already have been known. Some scholars have suggested that not all these beads originated in Egypt, but this remains uncertain.

3

Early Dynastic, Old Kingdom and First Intermediate Period

Diversification of forms

During the Early Dynastic and the Old Kingdom the focus of innovation was on forming technology rather than on glazing. The glaze of this period was mainly produced by efflorescence, as evidenced by the thinness of glaze in areas of surface which have been incised and by its poor durability and low degree of hardness.

No longer is modelling, combined with abrading, the only way of forming objects (though it is the most common), but moulding, forming around a rod or core and the application of a finely ground layer of quartz above a coarser one are also developed. This latter

9. (Left) Figurine of a baboon, in efflorescence-glazed faience, holding a cone on its knee. Protodynastic, from Hierakonpolis. Height 52 mm. (Courtesy of the Petrie Museum of Egyptian Archaeolgy, University College London. UC11002.)

10. (Right) Early Dynastic tile in the form of a reed mat. From Abydos, Osiris temple. Length 90 mm. (Courtesy of the Petrie Museum of Egyptian Archaeology, University College London. UC 35579.)

11. Tiles from the galleries below the Step Pyramid of Djoser at Saqqara: (above left) convex blue-green faience tile; (right) reverse of the tile showing incomplete efflorescence; (below) view showing the raised boss and pierced hole for threading on to a wire. Third Dynasty. Approximately 57 by 38 mm. (Courtesy of School of Archaeology, Classics and Oriental Studies, University of Liverpool. Objects E105, E101 and E103.)

technique has been observed on pieces from Hierakonpolis which otherwise have a brown sand and clay core.

By the Early Dynastic, votive figurines, known from Hierakonpolis, Elephantine and Abydos, were being made in the form of humans or animals. These are hand-modelled and fairly crude but represent the first move away from the use of faience mainly for beads.

In the manufacture of these small figurines, and other objects (figure 10) from various sites, distinct regional or workshop trends can be seen in terms of preferred colouring and shaping methods. At Abydos there is an early attempt at making polychrome faience by mixing two different coloured bodies together to give a marbleised effect.

The Djoser Step Pyramid complex makes use of some 36,000 blue-green glazed tiles each measuring approximately 60 by 35-40 mm (figure 11). These were made in a concave mould and the reverse side was abraded to leave a rectangular knob or boss, which was then drilled from both sides. The tiles were then threaded on copper wires and set in rows in plaster. Since the lengths of the tiles vary, it has also been suggested that they were partly formed by being rolled out between two sticks to define their width, and their length simply judged by eye. This, however, does not satisfactorily account for their convex surface and it is possible that many similar, but not exact, copies of the mould were in use to produce the many thousands of tiles required.

Perhaps the wires and the tiles were made in close proximity, since from some sites, such as Abydos and Beit Khallaf, analysis of the faience composition is echoed in that of copper artefacts, suggesting that the industries may be closely related. Even if the two activities were not carried out in the same workshop it is possible that the waste products from copper working were commonly used by faience workers.

At one time it was believed that faience underwent something of a decline in popularity during the Old Kingdom, and that its application at Saqqara, for the decorative tiles of Djoser, was its only major use, but this view has now been rectified. Czech excavations at Abusir, north of Saqqara, have produced large quantities of faience from the Fifth Dynasty mortuary complex of Raneferef and elsewhere (figures 12 and 13). These include blue tablets and inlays, the former of fine structure, which, as well as inscriptions, showed the king and deities. Details were inlaid in white paste and gold leaf, itself engraved. There were also inlays, probably from wooden vases, which have a coarse brown core overlaid by a fine white layer covered by black and bluish-green glaze. The technique of inlaying faience with paste of another colour may be related to the paste inlay technique known from the tomb of Nefermaat at Meydum dating to the Fourth Dynasty.

The First Intermediate Period did not mark any radical departure from the Old Kingdom methods of production, and some quite sophisticated work, including marbleising, is recorded.

12. Hieroglyphic signs from the pyramid complex of Khentkawes, south-east of the pyramid temple of Raneferef (Fifth Dynasty, time of Neferirkare/ Niuserre) at Abusir, excavated by the Czechoslovak Expedition. (Courtesy of Professor M. Verner, Czechoslovak Institute of Egyptology, Charles University.)

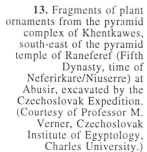

13. Fragments of plant ornaments from the pyramid complex of Khentkawes, south-east of the pyramid temple of Raneferef (Fifth Dynasty, time of Neferirkare/Niuserre) at Abusir, excavated by the Czechoslovak Expedition. (Courtesy of Professor M. Verner, Czechoslovak Institute of Egyptology, Charles University.)

4
Middle Kingdom and Second Intermediate Period

The expansion of faience working

With the re-establishment of order after the First Intermediate Period, faience manufacture apparently underwent an accelerated development and faience workers seem to have been particularly highly valued during the Middle Kingdom. This is suggested by the relatively rich burial given to one Debeni, an overseer of faience workers discovered in a shaft grave at Lisht and probably dating to the Thirteenth Dynasty.

Production may have been accelerated by the introduction of cementation glazing as a common method, a development attested at least as early as the reign of Sesostris I (Twelfth Dynasty). Middle Kingdom glazes are more durable and brighter than their forebears, and the body material can also be harder. Similarly, the core-forming of vessels, only an occasional practice in the Old Kingdom, now became common, as did the use of a fine layer of white quartz between glaze and core.

Animal figures were common in the Middle Kingdom and those approximating to spherical shapes were sometimes formed around a ball, or core, of straw. This applied particularly to the popular hedgehog figurines which are found in the shaft tombs of Beni Hasan and elsewhere and which may have symbolised the desert environment. Later the hedgehog form is used for making small jars which may have held magical-medicinal substances.

Hippopotamus figurines, usually decorated with aquatic plants, probably symbolised the revitalising properties of the Nile and were also common subjects for faience work at this time. Most decoration follows the contours of the body, adding to their overall effect, though they are occasionally undecorated. Their significance seems to have been religious and, in addition to symbolising the Nile, they may sometimes be associated with one of the forms of Seth. Found in burials of the Twelfth and, more especially, the Thirteenth Dynasty, they are placed in the coffin under the small of the back, under the feet or generally close to the body. They are widely known from Egypt and even occur as far south as Kerma in the Sudan.

Several animal figurines, presumably serving an amuletic function,

14. Figurine of a cat in faience. The glaze colour varies from turquoise to deep blue. From Abydos, tomb 416, late Twelfth or Thirteenth Dynasty. Length 71 mm. (Courtesy of School of Archaeology, Classics and Oriental Studies, University of Liverpool. Object E160.)

might occur in a single tomb, such as the group from Abydos tomb 416 comprising a lion, baboon, hedgehog and springing cat (figure 14). Many other species are known, including crocodiles, jerboa mice, frogs and baboons. Hand modelling was used in the production of many of these animal and human figurines, such as that of a resting dog or the very delicately modelled seated man holding a small oryx, both now in the Brooklyn Museum.

Female figurines ('Concubines of the Dead') were also produced by Middle Kingdom workers (figure 15). These figurines, often truncated at the knees, are associated with fertility and sexuality and as such are shown naked, though with elaborate wigs and jewellery, with the pubic triangle marked in black. They may also be patterned on their thighs and buttocks with what are believed to be tattoo marks. Such marks are actually known from bodies of two young women of this period from Thebes. This tattooing has often led to the appellation 'dancing girls' but there is no evidence for this supposition. The figures are sometimes shown holding a child, a further symbol of their fertility aspect. Like the animal figurines, these are found in tombs of both adults and children but also occur on settlement sites.

Funerary statuettes in faience can occur at this time too, though only rarely, and were probably made by a combination of moulding and hand modelling. Details are painted on.

Scarabs are well attested during the Middle Kingdom, though these are commonly steatite, often glazed. Perhaps this was preferred because of the clarity of inscribed detail when worked by the best hands. The stone is soft to work but hardens on firing as it converts to enstatite. It serves as a reminder that the glazing of other materials did not cease with the invention of faience.

Food offerings might also be made in faience for deposition in tombs. Popular subjects were beans, cucumbers, bunches of grapes, figs and sycamore figs, while meat can be represented by a calf (figure 16) and, in one case, by a pigeon. Likewise, tombs might be furnished with miniature faience vessels, which often copy full-size examples commonly made in pottery or other media.

Faience vessels of the Middle Kingdom can be thick-walled, but despite this many fine pieces were produced, such as bowls decorated with Nilotic scenes (figure 17). The overall decorative scheme of

15. Female figurines in faience, truncated at the knees. These are sometimes referred to as 'concubines' or 'brides of the dead'. Believed to come from Kahun town. Twelfth Dynasty. Height (left) 94 mm, (right) 78 mm. (Courtesy of the Petrie Museum of Egyptian Archaeology, University College London. UC 16725, 16726.)

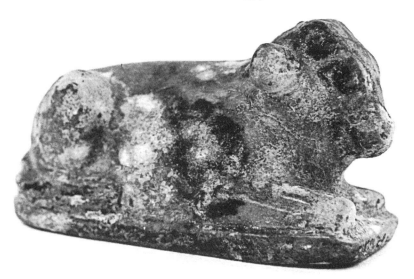

16. Figurine of recumbent calf in blue faience. From Harageh, tomb 353. Twelfth Dynasty. Length 57 mm. (Courtesy of the Petrie Museum of Egyptian Archaeology, University College London. UC 18744.)

water plants, sometimes with fish or birds, is reminiscent of the decoration applied to the hippopotami, which is not, perhaps, surprising since individual workshops probably produced a whole range of artefacts. Some of these bowls have better quality decoration on the inside than on the outside, and this tradition is also found on examples from succeeding periods.

Similarly, there are small saucer-like vessels with relatively simple water-lily decoration inside and out. Vessels often make use of an intermediate layer of fine quartz between glaze and core, as evidenced by some of the vessels from Abydos tomb 416. It has been found that such a layer is commonest where the core is not naturally white and that, as well as increasing reflectivity, it may serve to prevent iron, present in a brownish core, affecting the surface glaze.

During the Second Intermediate Period, bowls which probably served as drinking vessels developed. The lower part of the exterior is decorated with lotus petals, probably derived from the more elaborate lotus cups of the Middle Kingdom. The interiors of the vessels, however, carry scenes of marsh life showing lotus and papyrus plants, the *Tilapia* fish and water fowl. Both the *Tilapia* fish and the lotus were symbolic of rebirth and renewal. These themes become further developed in the New Kingdom.

Jars were also made in faience and, like some pottery vessels, may be decorated with skeuomorphs of netting, representing the bags or nets in which vessels were carried. The tall, beaker-like cylinder jars, derived from stone cosmetic jars, are also quite common in this period and are often good examples of the thick-walled type of faience so often encountered.

Faience production also flourished at Kerma in the Sudan, where jewellery and other products were made to standards comparable to those in Middle Kingdom Egypt. Various methods of production were in use, including application glazing, as evidenced by some tiles which show drip marks, which experiments have shown cannot be the result of the glaze running during firing. The inlaying of one faience paste into another, which develops in the New Kingdom, also first occurs at this site during the Second Intermediate Period. Faience manufacture continued in Egypt through this uncertain period and, by its end manufacturing methods were virtually fully developed.

17. Blue faience bowl with decoration of fish and marsh vegetation, in black. From Hu. Twelfth Dynasty. Diameter 130mm. (Courtesy of the Petrie Museum of Egyptian Archaeology, University College London. UC 18758.)

5

New Kingdom and Third Intermediate Period

Technological evidence

This period offers the student of faience and its technology a mass of information, much of it brought to light by W. M. Flinders Petrie in his excavations at Amarna, where he found several workshops producing faience and glass. Despite his account, many particulars remain unclear, though the work provides valuable evidence for the scale of production.

Illustrative of scale is Petrie's statement regarding the clay moulds, of which he 'brought nearly five thousand from Tell el-Amarna, after rejecting large quantities of the commonest: and these comprise over five hundred varieties' (figure 18). Such moulds are known from other sites too, including Malkata (the palace of Amenophis III at Thebes), Gurob and Qantir, from which Mahmud Hamza collected about ten thousand specimens. Lesser numbers occur on many sites and may suggest small-scale as well as factory production. They are made of fired clay and the underside frequently bears marks from the palm of the hand, while the upper surface has an

18. Faience moulds from Amarna: (above left) *Udjat* eye; (right) *Ankh;* (below left) ring shank; (below right) grapes. Length of *Udjat* eye, 35 mm. Eighteenth Dynasty. (Courtesy of the Egypt Exploration Society. Photograph Gwil Owen. Objects 7773, 7825, 7702, 7641.)

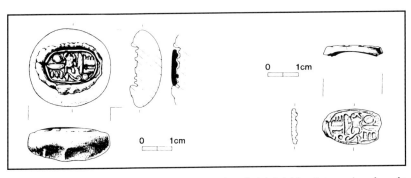

19. (Above left) Clay mould for making ring bezel; (right) blue faience bezel made from the mould. It is inscribed for Tutankhamun. Length of mould 27.25 mm. (Courtesy of the Egypt Exploration Society. Photograph: Gwil Owen. Amarna Objects 8761, 8762.) (Below) Detailed drawing of the mould and bezel. Eighteenth Dynasty. (Courtesy of the Egypt Exploration Society. Drawing: Andrew Boyce.)

impression of the object to be moulded. These moulds are always one-part or 'open-face' moulds so that one side of the object is always flat or secondarily shaped. It is one of the characteristics of this New Kingdom industry that moulding replaces modelling as the major method of shaping objects.

Andrew Boyce has produced a study of the manufacture of faience finger rings at Amarna which illustrates well the making and use of moulds (figures 18 and 19). First an impression of an existing ring bezel would be made in the wet clay intended for the mould. It was necessary to lift the bezel cleanly out of the clay since any overhang would later make the soft faience paste difficult to remove from the mould. Some moulds show an impression from a cord, which may have helped remove the master from the clay. An impression of a shank was made in a separate piece of clay, and finally the clay moulds were fired. After firing, the faience paste was pressed into the moulds, allowed to dry for some minutes and then removed. The bezels and shanks were then luted together using faience paste and allowed to dry fully. During drying, the salts would effloresce at the surface and on firing produce a glaze of the desired colour.

The mould could be used again, and Petrie describes finding a number of them choked with paste from the accumulated debris of multiple use. Several such moulds containing a powdery paste were discovered in the excavations of the Egypt Exploration Society in the 1980s and 1990s at Amarna, some with traces of colour preserved.

The luting together of individual elements is widely used to make fanciful cage arrangements of beads and especially to attach suspension loops to beads and amulets. This was probably a more efficient method of production than piercing the objects and may reflect the increased demand for faience at this time.

Petrie found no faience kilns at Amarna, though a square structure described as a charcoal-burning furnace, near the glazing works, was thought to be similar to a glass or faience kiln (figure 20). This is unproven, however, and little is known of faience kilns before Roman times.

From the so-called faience factory at Lisht come beads threaded on slender reeds, on which they were stored prior to firing, a technique which probably has a long ancestry.

The moulding of finger rings was facilitated by a new mixture of the faience paste. This used more alkali flux and sometimes included ground glass, which made it harder than earlier mixtures, so that the rings could be thinner than would previously have been possible.

The addition of glass to the faience body during the New Kingdom tends to support the view that this industry was conducted alongside glass making. Added glass can be difficult to differentiate from interstitial glass formed by the glazing methods. However, Professor M. S. Tite has found that sometimes the interstitial glass, like glass objects of the time, can contain cobalt but not copper while the glaze of the same piece contains copper not cobalt. In such cases, where the interstitial glass and surface glaze are different in composition, glass was most probably deliberately added to the body.

New colours were also developed, such as lemon-yellow and soft or light green (both produced using antimony and lead), violet or

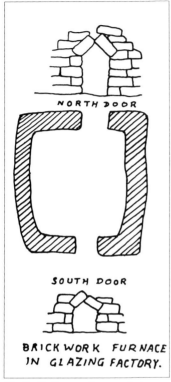

20. (Left) Furnace from a glazing workshop at Amarna measuring approximately 1950 by 1450 mm. Eighteenth Dynasty. (After Petrie, *Tell el-Amarna*, London, 1894, plate 42.)
21. (Right) Inscribed underside of a scarab. The green inlay, into a blue body, reads 'The Temple [called] glorious is Seti-Merneptah in the estate of Ptah'. Memphis. Nineteenth Dynasty. Height 77 mm. (Courtesy of the Petrie Museum of Egyptian Archaeology, University College London. UC 12591.)

purple (through the use of cobalt), red and opaque white, as well as combinations of colours to give a polychrome effect. Glass seems to have been added to some faience glazes, perhaps to enrich them and to extend their colour range.

The introduction of the glass industry gave a particular boost to the polychrome technique, and it is perhaps not coincidental that the use of both antimony and lead along with cobalt appears under Tuthmosis III, who is generally credited with establishing glass manufacture in Egypt. The lead antimonate used in making yellow faience and preparing yellow glass has been examined using isotope analyses and seems to have been derived from the Red Sea littoral

22. Daisy tile from Amarna. The background is in green faience, the daisies, made separately and inlaid, are in white and yellow. Late Eighteenth Dynasty. Length 51 mm. (Courtesy of the Petrie Museum of Egyptian Archaeology, University College London. UC 460.)

rather than imported from outside Egypt. So, even though lead antimonate appears at the same time as glass, and even though glass making may be established through foreign contact, it does seem that some local, rather than imported, materials were used in both faience and glass.

Scarabs (figure 21) commonly occur in faience at this time, and though many might be described as amuletic, and so are not dealt with in this book, some, such as that commemorating the marriage of Amenophis III and Tiye, are not. An example in the Brooklyn Museum is in violet-blue faience with the inscription clearly executed in bluish white pigment.

Faience tiles (figure 22) and other architectural ornaments increase too, notably at palaces such as Malkata, Amarna and Qantir, where numerous fragments of such inlays and decorations are known (figures

23. Polychrome faience inlays from Amarna showing a duck and a fish. The reverse of these delicate pieces shows textile impressions. Late Eighteenth Dynasty. The duck is 45 mm wide, the fish 51 mm. (Courtesy of the Petrie Museum of Egyptian Archaeology, University College London. UC 509, U.C 406.)

 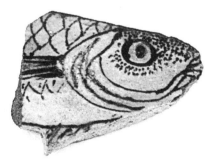

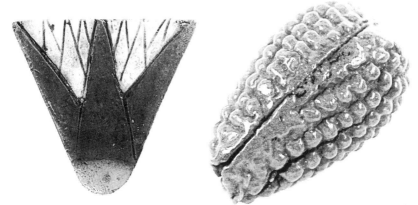

24. (Left) Lotus inlay in polychrome faience from Amarna. Height 63 mm. Eighteenth Dynasty. (Courtesy of the Petrie Museum of Egyptian Archaeology, University College London. UC 907 and 909.)

25. (Right) A blue faience grape cluster, made in two parts and then joined. Such pieces could be of considerable size. Amarna. Eighteenth Dynasty. Length 40 mm. (Courtesy of the Petrie Museum of Egyptian Archaeology, University College London. UC 23267.)

23 and 24). These include cartouche rings, hieroglyphs and figures. Bunches of grapes, well known from Amarna, may have been hung from the ceilings of some rooms, and clusters made with one flat side attached to walls or pillars, the whole giving the effect of a trellised vineyard (figure 25). Many of these inlays are made by the efflorescence method, as is clear from the poor glazing of the reverse side. This side may also show marks left from resting the pieces on cloth whilst they dried after removal from the mould (figure 26).

The tiles from Medinet Habu and from Qantir showing foreign prisoners are especially fine. Those from the palace of the mortuary temple of Ramesses III (Medinet Habu) show the racial characteristics of each prisoner, along with their colourful costumes, in great detail, the polychrome work being of the highest order. The reverses of these pieces show

26. Textile impression on the reverse of a green faience tile from Amarna. Faience commonly seems to have been put on sheets of textile during drying. Length 29 mm. Eighteenth Dynasty. (Courtesy of the Egypt Exploration Society. Photograph: Gwil Owen. Object 21118.)

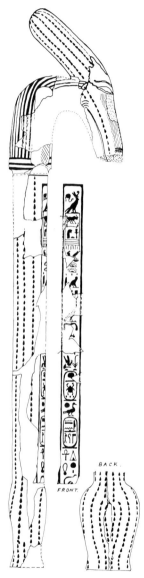

manufacturers' marks. The use of faience as inlay on smaller objects is common at this time.

Faience could itself be inlaid. This was not a new technique, but it was characteristic of the New Kingdom factories to inlay one kind of faience with another once the first piece had begun to dry so that the two parts would shrink away from one another slightly, thus leaving a small void around the added colour.

New Kingdom faience often comprised high-quality work not only in small objects but also in large pieces such as the faience lions from Qantir and the huge *was* sceptre inscribed in manganese for Amenophis II, found by Petrie at Naqada in 1894 (figure 27). The stem of this was made in short sections joined together with paste and fired so that the glaze covered the whole evenly. The head had also been manufactured separately. The sceptre and the lions are the largest objects of faience work known.

Bowls are common products of the New Kingdom. They are generally of blue faience with black designs, which vary in quality, and it is common for the interior designs to be better executed than the exterior, suggesting that two different hands were at work, one of which might be that of an apprentice. The form is derived from deeper vessels of the Second Intermediate Period, the outside frequently being decorated with a lotus flower while the inside bears decoration showing marsh scenes, fish and the Hathor head or cow, all motifs suggesting regeneration. They may have served for offering water. Hathor and Bastet (with whom she is identified) are the only deities

27. *Was* sceptre found by Petrie at Nubt (Naqada) in 1894. Made in sections, this is one of the largest faience objects known. Length 2158 mm. (After Petrie, *Naqada and Ballas*, London, 1895, plate 78. Victoria and Albert Museum number 437-1895.)

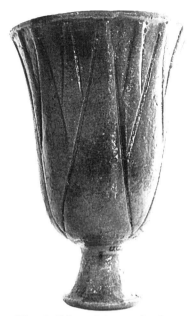

28. (Above) Sherd from a bowl showing the face of Hathor, one of whose epithets was 'Lady of Faience'. Provenance unknown. Eighteenth or Nineteenth Dynasty. Length 67 mm. (Courtesy of the Petrie Museum of Egyptian Archaeology, University College London. UC 38094.)

29. (Right) Blue faience lotus chalice, from Ramesses II's rebuilding of the temple of Seth at Naqada (Nubt). Nineteenth Dynasty. Height 135 mm. (Courtesy of the Petrie Museum of Egyptian Archaeology, University College London. UC 15891.)

named on the vessels (figure 28). Fragments of these bowls are known from Hathor shrines and temples at Deir el-Bahri, Faras in Nubia and at Serabit el-Khadim in Sinai, where she is referred to as 'lady of turquoise'. Elsewhere she is referred to as 'lady of faience', indicating her special association with turquoise and its substitute, faience. Such bowls are less common in domestic contexts, though the later types may be for domestic use. After the Eighteenth Dynasty their popularity declines and their decoration becomes less elaborate. The external decoration is lost, while scenes of the marshes are replaced by the white lotus, animals and humans, some bearing offerings.

Faience chalices appear from the start of the Eighteenth Dynasty and represent both the blue and the white lotus flower (figure 29). Those representing the blue lotus were known as *seshen* and are the most common, while Edward Brovarksi suggests that the rarer white lotus form may have served as a stately drinking vessel from the Amarna period onwards. The lotus is a symbol of rebirth and may also be associated with Hathor, in which case the faience material may have been of particular significance. The early chalices are

Egyptian Faience and Glass

30. Egyptian copy of a Mycenaean stirrup jar in blue faience. Unprovenanced. Eighteenth Dynasty, time of Amenophis III. Maximum diameter 67 mm. (Courtesy of the Petrie Museum of Egyptian Archaeology, University College London. UC 16630.)

rather heavy with wide mouths and thick walls. The stems are low and the thick, dark glaze has often run deep into the grooves of the decoration. The later examples are more delicate, with details of the leaves sometimes being shown. The latest examples are more slender and trumpet-shaped, with delicate relief and details on both leaves and petals.

A study of an early example from Abydos, now in the Museum of Fine Arts, Boston, illustrates the maker's skill. The piece was made in two parts, the upper cup being formed in a concave mould and the base probably around a rod, which was then used to flare it to make the foot. The two halves were then joined with faience paste. The pieces were still soft as this was done so that the cup does not sit true on the base but is rather tilted. Once dry, the relief was carved into the vessel, cutting away some of the effloresced salts, which necessitated dipping the vessel in a slurry of white quartz and alkali with copper to give a layer 0.5 mm thick. Air bubbles formed along the lines of parts of the pattern and afterwards the edges of the decoration and the bands at top and bottom of the cup were reworked. In firing, the applied layer did not thoroughly wet the underlying body where there had been reworking or air bubbles, so that the glaze crawled, a common fault in faience. Nonetheless, like many in its class, this is a particularly fine vessel.

A vessel from Serabit el-Khadim should also be mentioned here, since it is thought to be wheel-thrown, a rare technique at this time and not well developed until later.

Egyptian faience objects were exported to Cyprus and elsewhere in the Mediterranean as well as to the Near East, notably to Byblos in the Lebanon during the Nineteenth Dynasty.

Vessels also imitate foreign forms such as biconical flasks or stirrup jars (figure 30) copied from Aegean types, though often with locally inspired decoration. Mycenaean pottery was imported into Egypt at this time and is well known from sites such as Amarna.

By the Third Intermediate Period faience technology was spreading widely in the Mediterranean so that local copies of Egyptian products can be difficult to differentiate from the original products even with the use of chemical analyses. There are chemical changes to the Egyptian faience of this time, however, and antimony and cobalt, introduced in the New Kingdom, virtually disappear, though tin and lead remain quite common. Nonetheless, the tin concentrations in faience had been declining since the end of the Ramesside era and this decline is mirrored by the concentrations observed in bronze artefacts of this time, illustrating a general decline in the use of tin and, perhaps, further demonstrating a link between the faience and metallurgy industries.

The faience of the Twenty-second Dynasty frequently shows brown spots, which may have been deliberately produced. In this same period glassy faience appears, resembling precious stones in its shininess. It was formerly thought of as a Twenty-sixth Dynasty innovation. It may have become a substitute for glass, which declines at this time. Glassy faience is produced until Roman times, though its use in vessel manufacture seems to be limited to the Ptolemaic period.

Most characteristic of Third Intermediate Period faience products were chalices, decorated with registers in relief, and numerous shabtis in turquoise-blue with black inscriptions. Large sets of shabtis of various types, along with overseer figures, were produced (figure 31). Plaques are also found.

31. Deep blue faience shabti of Pinedjem I, details in black. This High Priest of Amun came to rule as 'King' in the Theban area, hence the remains of a uraeus on his brow. Provenance unknown. Twenty-first Dynasty. (Courtesy of the Petrie Museum of Egyptian Archaeology, University College London. UC 39860.)

32. (Above) Hathor head from a *naos sistrum*. The matt-finished piece is double-sided and the workmanship is exceptionally fine. Provenance unknown. Twenty-sixth Dynasty. Height 62 mm. (Courtesy of the Petrie Museum of Egyptian Archaeology, University College London. UC 5282.)

33. (Right) Shabti with inscription for User-pa-haty. Provenance unknown. Thirtieth Dynasty. Height 130 mm. (Courtesy of the Petrie Museum of Egyptian Archaeology, University College London. UC 19659.)

34. (Left) Figurine of Thoth in effloresced green faience. The work is particularly fine. There are loops for suspension at each side of the head. Memphis, palace of Apries. Persian Period. Height 119 mm. (Courtesy of the Petrie Museum of Egyptian Archaeology, University College London. UC 30110.)

6
The Late Period and after

Revival

The Twenty-sixth Dynasty revival under the Saites of traditional Egyptian art led to new developments in faience. Amongst these was the appearance of a characteristic apple-green faience which was used for shabtis, pilgrim flasks and votive offerings, the most popular of which seem to have been model *sistra* emblems of Hathor. This Saite faience is of better quality than that of the Third Intermediate Period, with better control of colour and more durable glazes. Some of the innovations of the New Kingdom and Third Intermediate period declined; for example, matt faience (figure 32) seems to have been preferred over glossy, and polychrome work was less frequent and, where attempted, the colours were overlaid rather than inlaid.

Antimony was again used and its return brought back true yellow glazes, though the green, which also uses antimony, is more characteristic. Shades of green were carefully prepared using varying proportions of lead and antimony, though this technique may well have been confined to workshops under state patronage, since much of the green glaze made at other establishments still used copper as a colorant. Iron concentrations also increased at this time.

The mass production of shabti figures continued and, following a development at the end of the Third Intermediate Period, these were now moulded and the inscriptions incised rather than painted on (figure 33). The glazing of these, and other, figurines was by efflorescence or by cementation and the quality is often high (figure 34).

Black glaze increased in popularity during the Late Period, but instead of using manganese, kiln conditions were manipulated to produce a reducing atmosphere. This technique keeps iron oxides in their reduced state, imparting a black colour to the glaze. Kaczmarczyk and Hedges have suggested that this change in technique might have resulted from contact with Carian Greek mercenaries and their compatriots who served in Egypt during the Twenty-sixth Dynasty and were settled at Naucratis. The Greeks of this period were expert in the manipulation of iron-rich clays to produce black colouring, though the Egyptian potters were familiar with the technique from early times. This was a radical change from earlier faience practice, though it was more common in Lower

Egypt, the south of the country maintaining the use of manganese for black colouring for somewhat longer.

That a link between metallurgy and faience production existed is again suggested by the correlation between amounts of tin in bronze and faience from different parts of Egypt. In areas with low concentrations of tin in bronze the amount in faience is similarly low, and *vice versa.*

The faience of this revival period could be excellent, both in the execution of the pieces and in the perfection of the glaze, which, when not matt, can resemble glass.

Much of this Late Period faience was exported, such as the so-called 'New Year flasks' which were traded all over the Mediterranean. These probably contained perfumes and were made to mark New Year festivals. They are of lentoid form with two handles on the side and may have elaborate relief decoration.

The Ptolemaic and Roman industry is not fully documented, though some production sites are known. Those in the Delta used natron as a source of alkali, although, surprisingly, Memphis seems to have continued with a tradition established in the Predynastic: the higher potassium levels recorded in its faience are more characteristic of the use of plant ashes, though contemporary glass makers at the site were using natron.

The use at this time of the difficult technique of wheel-throwing faience perhaps reflects a link between the faience and potting industries.

Memphis provides the first clear evidence of actual faience kilns, though of Roman date. They are square with vertical sides, are both large and deep, and are probably evidence of large-scale production. There is no evidence of a perforated kiln floor and the vessels were fired in saggars amongst which the fuel was thrown. The kiln stoke hole was positioned approximately halfway up the kiln.

Inside the saggars, vessels were inverted on three-pointed stands and then had little pottery cones stuck to their bases with soft clay. On these went the next dish and so on until the saggar was full. Clay would be used to lute one saggar to the base of the next one, so keeping the furnace gases out of the vessel but allowing the heat to fire the contents.

Petrie described finding balls or pills of blue glaze which had been fritted and would eventually be ground up to form the basis of the glaze. This would be applied either as a powder or as a slurry.

Polychrome faience was popular, though yellow was frequently

35. Finely detailed lid showing Horus. This piece is of fine workmanship, though faience at this time lacks much of the colour of earlier pieces. Probably from Memphis. Ptolemaic. Diameter 40 mm. (Courtesy of the Petrie Museum of Egyptian Archaeology, University College London. UC 33516.)

used as the background colour. Cobalt was used again during this period in the making of violet and indigo glazes and, along with iron, in the making of black glaze, again at the expense of manganese.

Late in the Ptolemaic period (figure 35) and into the early Roman, the range of colours used was less flamboyant than earlier in the period, and the industry lacked much of its earlier creativity.

PART II: GLASS
7
The material and its technology

The origin and development of glass

According to Pliny the Elder (AD 23/24-79) glass making was discovered when a group of merchants, probably *en route* from Egypt, put ashore beside the mouth of the river Belus in Phoenicia (now the river Na'aman in Israel). Unable to find sufficient stones on which to rest their cauldrons over the cooking fire, they used some of the lumps of natron they were carrying as cargo. The following morning it was noticed that these stones had melted and their reaction with the sand had produced a shiny, vitreous material like an artificial stone. So was glass discovered.

Though historically incorrect, Pliny's account covers some of the essential elements of glass composition. The material is composed mainly of silica, alkali and lime. Silica was obtained from sand, crushed flint or quartz. The silica is the network former for glass but, in order to melt it at sufficiently low temperatures, ancient workers found it necessary to add a network modifier in the form of alkali. This served as a flux in the process.

Alkalis were added in the form of plant ashes, particularly from the burning of salt-marsh plants, or as natron. Ancient texts (from Assyria and, later, from Classical times — there are no Pharaonic accounts) do not mention the addition of lime and it must be supposed that this was generally present as an impurity in sand, a property which doubtless made some sand deposits more highly prized for glass making than others. Such sands occur at the mouth of the Belus, perhaps inspiring Pliny's story.

Alkali consists of carbonates which react with the silica to make sodium silicate and carbon dioxide. In a modern furnace the temperature is $1550°C$ and the glass is relatively fluid so that the carbon dioxide is liberated and leaves no bubbles in the glass. Ancient glass furnaces, however, could achieve only about $1000°C$, and though this would be sufficient to melt the raw ingredients it would not be enough to reduce their viscosity sufficiently to allow the gas bubbles (*seed*) which developed to escape and the unmelted lumps of raw material (*stones*) to settle out. Ancient glass making was therefore a two-stage process.

The first stage, known as *fritting*, involved the heating together of the raw materials at a temperature between 700 and 850°C until they formed a mass resembling partly melted sugar. The mixture of sand and plant ash was constantly kept in contact by continual raking, which also prevents the formation of semi-liquids. If 850°C is exceeded the mixture becomes sugary and begins to melt, whereupon carbon dioxide is trapped. The continual raking during this solid-state reaction leaves a dry sodium silicate. To assist in further reducing the necessary temperatures, the Egyptians used a higher proportion of alkali than do modern glass makers, which rendered their glass softer and less resistant to weathering. On cooling, a solidified mass remained, the lower part comprising the unmelted sediment, the middle fraction a crystallised glass material, and the upper part a vesicular mass. The impurities were chipped away from the lower surface, as were any in the upper layer, and the remaining material was crushed into a fine glass powder.

This sodium silicate powder could then be melted at a higher temperature, up to *c*.1000°C, to produce molten glass (sometimes called the *metal*) which would be relatively free of gas bubbles. This could then be formed. The glass would not be clear but would have some greenish or brownish discoloration from impurities such as iron in the sand, and numerous small bubbles, the result of incomplete fusion, would remain. To achieve a clear glass, or more commonly a coloured glass, additional agents were needed.

Clear glass is known by the Eighteenth Dynasty. To make it, a decoloriser was used. This was, perhaps, manganese oxide, which frequently occurs in ancient Egyptian glass, though not usually in large enough amounts to cause decolorisation. Interestingly, some of the earliest clear glass contains no antimony or manganese, so that the decoloriser is unknown.

Manganese was also used to modify the blue colours produced by the copper or cobalt, so commonly used by the Egyptians. For a long time it was believed that cobalt must have been imported to Egypt from Iraq or Iran, but, although it does not seem to have a source in the Nile Valley, it has been found in the Eastern Desert and in the Dakhleh and Kharga Oases. Since it is such a strong colorant it is needed only in tiny quantities, often so small that they are hard to detect even with modern analytical equipment.

Copper was used to produce green glass and, in association with manganese, it could make black, though this could also result from a high proportion of iron compounds. At first, black may have been produced unintentionally, but by the peak of the industry it was deliberately made. The addition of tin oxide or calcium antimonate rendered glass an opaque white, the opacity being the more apparent owing to the numerous tiny bubbles inherent in the glass and, on vessels, by the presence of traces of the core around which they were formed being left inside (see below). Red was produced using red oxide of copper under reducing (low oxygen) conditions, while yellow derived from the use of antimony or iron compounds.

How many of these ingredients were recognised as substances in their own right, were thought of as particular sands or occurred as traces in other materials (so that it was these other materials which were thought to impart the desired colour) is unknown. However, we can be certain that the early glass makers carefully observed the results of their work and were able to reproduce effects using the same raw materials without necessarily knowing why they achieved given results.

The glass could now be prepared for use. A core might be dipped into the molten mass, or semi-liquid glass might be poured on to the core. Alternatively, the glass could be poured to form *rods*, which in turn could be rolled to make *canes* which could be softened for later use. The glass might be allowed to solidify as a block, for later cold cutting, or be moulded. The techniques used and their frequency are discussed below.

8

The earliest glass in Egypt

Early occurrences

Despite the early use of glaze and faience in Egypt, glass as a material in its own right, rather than as glaze, appears relatively late, the most securely dated examples appearing only in the New Kingdom. However, recent work is tending to suggest the introduction of glass, albeit as an import, at ever earlier dates.

Glass is an artificial product and, like faience, was used to imitate semi-precious stones. It had sufficient intrinsic value to be a gift suitable for the highest nobility and was itself imitated in less costly materials. It has been suggested that glass was developed only when it was appreciated in its own right, rather than as an interesting accident of faience making, and that once this stage was reached the technology, using molten material and adding colorants sometimes derived from metal working (copper was perhaps added as hammer-scale), owed more to metallurgy than to faience making, where the shapes are formed cold. However, finds from various sites, including Amarna, suggest that glass and faience making went on in close proximity and several crafts may have co-existed.

Its use as a substitute for semi-precious stones is reflected by the words used to refer to it, which are often the names of such stones, and occasionally even *thenet,* which is more correctly faience, is used. The most common names for the substance, however, are not Egyptian but are taken from Hurrian and Akkadian (ancient languages of Anatolia and Mesopotamia). These are the terms *ehlipakku* and *mekku* respectively. The use of these foreign names in texts of the New Kingdom may reflect the exotic origin of glass.

However, there are a few pieces of glass from Egypt which apparently pre-date the New Kingdom. They may be imports or result from accidents in glazing or faience making and many are still contentious. Those given here are only the most secure or most frequently cited.

A number of beads and amulets dating between the Fifth and Eleventh Dynasties are known, though most have not been subject to recent examination and so should be treated with extreme caution.

There are two scarabs, both inscribed for officials, one in opaque blue glass, the other in turquoise blue, which seem to be securely dated to the Twelfth Dynasty. The same applies to some so-called 'crumb-beads' of the same date which, according to J. D. Cooney, 'establish the occasional production of glass in the Middle Kingdom'.

Particularly controversial is the bull 'mosaic' from the treasure of Princess Khnumet found at Dahshur, dated to the Twelfth Dynasty. The 'mosaic', now in the Cairo Museum, has a covering now believed to be of rock crystal so that the underlying material cannot be examined, though it is probably paint rather than glass. Also of this date are a glass frog set in a silver ring and several eyes from funerary masks.

A glass rod with the cartouche of the Twelfth Dynasty king Amenemhat III, in the Egyptian Museum, Berlin, is probably a Roman piece since this king was commonly regarded as a deity in later times, and if we discount the bull 'mosaic' then the mosaic-glass technique is not encountered again until some time between the first century BC and the first century AD.

A glass inlay in a lotus flower pendant may be of Middle Kingdom date but, since the pendant has been re-strung using other pieces of jewellery and has no certain provenance, the date must be regarded as uncertain. The piece is in the British Museum collection.

A frequently cited lion's head amulet inscribed for Nubkheperre, and thought to refer to Nubkheperre In(yo)tef of the Seventeenth Dynasty, is being examined at the British Museum and its identification as glass is uncertain; it may date from as late as the Third Intermediate Period.

Although some of the pieces mentioned remain controversial, there are some examples of glass in Egypt from before the New Kingdom. It is worth reiterating, since references persist in the literature, that the Middle Kingdom tomb scenes showing men with blowpipes working over a fire represent copper workers not glass blowers. Blown glass is unknown in Egypt before the Roman period.

9

The New Kingdom

A fully fledged industry

This period represents the peak of ancient Egyptian glass working achievement, with production of a series of carefully crafted vessels, often of a high technical and artistic standard (figures 36 and 37), as well as inlays and other simpler pieces. Apart from those pieces discussed in chapter 8 there does not seem to be any period of experiment with glass: it arrives, apparently fully fledged, in the New Kingdom.

A square bead, now in the Museum of Fine Arts, Boston, of unknown provenance and in light-blue glass, bears on one side the name of Ahmose and on the other that of Amenophis I, the first two kings of the New Kingdom. If the bead is contemporary with them, then it pre-dates the established rise of glass making in Egypt by some fifty or sixty years.

The earliest fragments of vessels come from the tomb of Tuthmosis I and comprise two sherds of blue glass decorated with white, yellow and blue; these are possibly intrusive since this king was reburied in the reign of Hatshepsut. If so, then this may help to explain why little glass is known until the reign of Tuthmosis III, when production becomes firmly established and on a significant scale.

This sudden appearance of glass production is perhaps related to the campaigns of Tuthmosis III in the land of Mitanni (Upper Syria) when glass makers may have been brought to Egypt as captives. Some support for foreign craftsmen working in Egypt is found in the use of the non-Egyptian words *ehlipakku* and *mekku* by Egyptian scribes. The words were, until recently, translated as 'precious stone' but, though this is not entirely incorrect, it does not render their true sense. It has been shown from the Amarna letters that the two words are equivalent terms and that it is always the Egyptian king who requests these stones from foreign rulers. A reference in a later Assyrian text makes it clear that *mekku* is raw glass and that the 'precious stone' sought must therefore have been the raw material for glass making, probably as ingots.

This makes good sense if craftsmen were brought into Egypt, since they might require materials from their homelands in order to continue their craft satisfactorily.

A series of cylindrical blue glass 'columns', of uncertain provenance and now in various American and British museums, were thought

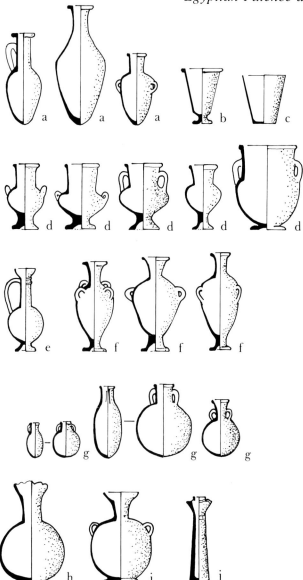

36. New Kingdom core-formed glass vessel forms of the Eighteenth and Nineteenth Dynasties: a, flasks; b, stemmed beakers; c, kohl pots; d, *krateriskoi*; e, base ring jugs; f, *amphoriskoi*; g, lentoid flasks; h, pomegranate flasks; i, jars; j, kohl tubes. (Courtesy of the Toledo Museum of Art. After Grose, *Early Ancient Glass*, New York, 1989, figure 23.)

37. Egyptian core-formed glass amphora with dark blue body and decoration in turquoise-blue around the lip and thread pattern in yellow and white. From Abydos. Second half of Eighteenth Dynasty. Height 98 mm. (Courtesy of the Pilkington Glass Museum. Object 1972/16.)

to be ancient ingots, but it has been suggested that these were part of a mosque frieze and may date from as late as the nineteenth century AD. However, this does not destroy the notion of the import of glass to Egypt, since from the Ulu Burun shipwreck off the Turkish coast, and dating to roughly the time of Amenophis III, come blue glass ingots which match contemporary Egyptian and Mycenaean glass in composition (figures 38 and 39). (It is, however, possible that these ingots were coming from Egypt.)

The import of raw materials, particularly early on in the production of glass, may explain why a name bead of Hatshepsut and one of Senenmut in clear glass, now in the British Museum, are compositionally similar to analyses of glass of a century later from Tell el-Amarna. The fact that clear glass could be produced at such an early date shows the technical skill of the early workers and also emphasises that the Egyptians did not need to colour their glass but rather that this was a matter of choice.

It is thought that glass probably remained a royal monopoly for much of the New Kingdom, and its frequent mention in diplomatic correspondence emphasises that it was of interest to royalty well into the period. Similarly, the provision of imitation glass vessels, made in painted wood, in tombs of even privileged persons, such as Huya and Thuya, shows that supply must always have been relatively limited. Stone vessels are also imitated in wood, and this may emphasise the view that glass was a kind of artificial stone, prized in its own right.

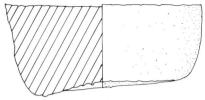

38. (Above) Blue glass ingot number KW3 from the Ulu Burun shipwreck, off the Turkish coast. The wreck of this vessel is a fascinating source of information on trade at this period, approximately contemporary with the reign of Amenophis III. Maximum diameter 154 mm, weight 2343 grams. (Courtesy of Professor G. F. Bass. After Bass, *American Journal of Archaeology*, 1986, 90, pages 269-96.)

39. (Above right) Blue glass ingot (inverted) from the Ulu Burun shipwreck. Diameter approximately 154 mm. (Photograph by Donald A. Frey/Institute of Nautical Archaeology.)

A number of glass workshops are known from the New Kingdom, notably from Malkata, a palace temple complex of Amenophis III at Thebes, and from Tell el-Amarna, the new capital city of the so-called heretic Pharaoh Akhenaten (Amenophis IV). Workshops

40. (Left) Cylindrical vessel used in glass-making as a support for bowls and in some cases as a crucible. Surface find from Amarna. Height 100 mm. Eighteenth Dynasty. (Courtesy of the Egypt Exploration Society. Photograph: Gwil Owen.)

41. (Below) Fritting pans supported on cylindrical vessels, themselves sometimes used as crucibles for glass making. The reconstruction is by Petrie based on evidence from the Amarna glazing workshops. (After Petrie, *Tell el-Amarna*, London, 1894, plate 13.)

Fritting Pans,
supported in the
furnace on jars
inverted, down
which the glaze runs.

W.M.F.P.

42. Fragment of cylindrical vessel used as a crucible in glass-making. The adhering material is dark blue glass. Surface find from the so-called 'Palace dumps' at Amarna. Length approximately 140 mm. Eighteenth Dynasty. (Courtesy of the Egypt Exploration Society. Photograph: Gwil Owen.)

of the Twentieth Dynasty are known from Lisht and Menshiyeh. At Amarna several workshops are known and it is possible that not all of these were under direct royal control. It has been found that samples of glass from Amarna and Malkata were coloured using cobalt, a sample from Lisht with copper. This might suggest that only the royal workshops had access to cobalt, though further work is needed.

A distinction should be drawn between glass making and glass working. If all raw material was supplied in the form of foreign ingots then the Egyptians would merely have worked these rather than have made glass from its raw materials. It is possible that some of the workshops at Amarna simply worked glass supplied by other manufactories or from abroad. However, Amarna may have been a turning point in glass making with some workshops producing their own glass from local raw materials.

At Amarna, Petrie discovered shallow saucer-shaped pans which he believed were for fritting raw materials; these probably stood on inverted cylindrical vessels, whose external sides and bases show clear runs of glass (figures 40 and 41). He also inferred the existence of smaller vessels used to melt the ground product of fritting for producing either larger ingots or working directly. The inference was based on the shape and size of pieces of glass which had cooled in these vessels and taken their form. The cylindrical supporting vessels may also have been used as melting pans in their own right, along with still larger crucibles, since a mass of glass of over 5000 cc is known and this could not have been produced in any vessel of the sizes found (figure 42). Pebbles of white quartz seem to have lined the Amarna furnace floors and to have been shattered by continual heating so that they could be ground up as high-quality silica.

43. Glass-working fragments from Amarna. The glass rod shows marks from rolling on a textured surface such as wood or stone. The blobs of glass show the marks of pincers with which they were removed from the batch. Late Eighteenth Dynasty. Length of rod 38 mm. (Courtesy of the Petrie Museum of Egyptian Archaeology, University College London. UC 22889A [rod], UC 22923.)

Numerous pieces of glass bearing the impression of tongs are known from Amarna, showing how samples of the glass were picked from the molten batch and examined. Some of the melted glass seems to have been poured, or perhaps pulled, from the crucible to make rods of varying thickness, while other rods were rolled thin to make glass rod or cane of more or less uniform thickness (figure 43).

Sufficient workshops and products are known to allow scholars such as Birgit Nolte to identify individual chronological *Werkkreise* or workshop groups.

After this peak of activity in the Eighteenth and Nineteenth Dynasties glass making declines from late in the Twentieth Dynasty but lingers on a reduced scale into the Twenty-first and beyond.

Core forming
Much New Kingdom glass production went to make delicate, often ornamented, vessels. These were not blown or moulded but core-formed (figure 44).

In this technique a core, corresponding to the shape of the vessel interior, was made of dung/vegetable matter mixed with clay and sand and formed around a wooden handle. The outside might also be given a coating of ground limestone mixed with ferruginous clay.

This core was either dipped into molten glass or had semi-molten material trailed over it, coil fashion. This was then rolled on a *marver,* a flat surface of stone or metal, to smooth the vessel walls and even their thickness. Trails of coloured glass could then be added from softening prepared pieces of glass cane. In the New Kingdom these were carefully applied and pulled or dragged to make swags around the vessel. The vessel was then rolled again on the marver to impress (marver-in) the pattern. Handles and bases could be worked separately, using pincers, and added to the main body once shaped, although rims and bases could also be drawn from the body material.

The finished vessel was then slowly cooled, a process known as *annealing,* to allow the stresses developed in the glass to be released gradually. A glass object which is cooled too rapidly will shatter or crack after a period of time. Once cool, the handling piece, which protruded through the vessel mouth, was removed and the core broken up a bit at a time and removed through this same opening. The opacity exhibited by many Egyptian vessels often

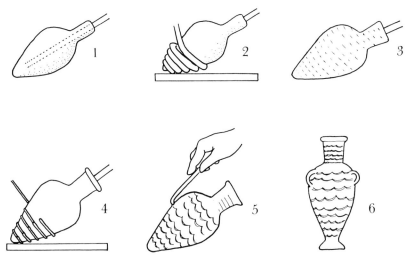

44. Stages in making a core-formed glass vessel, based on experimental work. 1. The core with handling piece. 2. Glass threads are wound around the core and marvered. 3. The piece once marvered. 4. Decorative threads are trailed on to the vase, and a glass cane is added to the rim. 5. The trails are feathered. 6. The finished product, with handles added. (Courtesy of the Toledo Museum of Art. After Grose, *Early Ancient Glass,* New York, 1989, figure 4.)

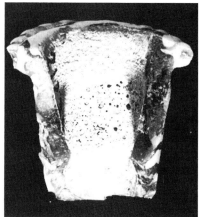

45. (Left) Decorated neck of core-formed vessel. The rim band is in yellow and brown, the body colour is dark blue with white, yellow and turquoise swags. (Right) Interior of neck showing bubbles where the glass was in contact with the core. This adds to the opacity of the piece. The marvered-in threads are also visible in the section. Diameter 16 mm. From Amarna. Eighteenth Dynasty. (Courtesy of the Egypt Exploration Society. Photograph: Gwil Owen. Object 21221.)

results from the incomplete removal of this core, especially under the shoulders of vessels (figure 45). The exterior of the vessel might also be polished after cooling to remove blemishes.

Irrespective of whether the glass was made by foreign or by Egyptian workers, the forms were to Egyptian taste, though shapes unique to glass were not developed. Rather, those common in other media were produced.

Amongst the earliest pieces of core-formed glass is a vase or jug in the British Museum, bearing the inscription 'For the good god Menkhepere (Tuthmosis III), given life'. This, a *nehenem* vase, was one of a set of seven jugs for sacred oils and must surely have come from the funerary equipment of the king. It is in a turquoise-blue glass with the inscription in yellow. This is often erroneously described as enamel but is made up of ground yellow glass fused on to the vessel, illustrating the great technical competence already exhibited at this early stage. It is the earliest example of this technique so far known anywhere. The vessel, only 87 mm high, is decorated with lines, dots and tamarisk trees.

Two chalices inscribed for this same king, are also known, one in the Munich collection (figure 46), the other, a gold-mounted example, in the Metropolitan Museum of Art, New York. Similar vessels bearing other royal names, particularly those of Amenophis II also exist.

Three types of core-formed vessel are especially numerous in the New Kingdom. The first is a two-handled jar, or *krateriskos* (figure 36 d), with a wide neck, of which some excellent examples exist. The British Museum possesses an especially fine example in opaque dark-blue glass, the neck decorated in opaque white and the body festooned in yellow and turquoise blue. The shape is clearly derived from stone ointment containers. The wide neck facilitated complete removal of the core so that these vessels appear to be especially translucent.

The second form is the lentoid flask (figures 47 and 36 g), commonly found in pottery and stone. The British Museum has a fine example, dating to the reign of Ramesses II, in translucent amethyst glass with a rim cord made separately in amethyst and white. Such prefabricated rim bands are common on this type of vessel. The two handles are opaque turquoise blue overlaid in threads of yellow and blue.

Third is the ubiquitous kohl tube, a tall cylindrical vessel, sometimes with out-turned rim made to resemble palm leaves so that the body forms the palm trunk, and used for containing eye make-up (figure 36 j). These are especially common in the Eighteenth and Nineteenth Dynasties. Such vessels would originally have had teardrop-shaped glass applicator rods, some of which still survive. The commonest use of glass vessels at this time was for storing and applying cosmetics.

Most core-formed vessels are closed forms, though there are

Yellow

Dark blue

Turquoise blue

46. Glass chalice inscribed for Tuthmosis III. This is a clear example of the mastery of glass from an early stage and perhaps suggests the bringing of foreign craftsmen to Egypt. Provenance unknown. Late Eighteenth Dynasty. (Drawing by Kate M. Trott. Munich Ä S 630.)

47. Dark blue glass pilgrim flask, with black and white rim with yellow band. Provenance unknown. Late Eighteenth or Nineteenth Dynasty. Height 112 mm. (Courtesy of the Petrie Museum of Egyptian Archaeology, University College London. UC 22081.)

occasional open forms, including the earliest footed bowl, which dates to the reign of Amenophis II. Generally these small core-formed vessels show no trace of a lid when found, though some have linen or wax stoppers. However, some vessels did originally have glass lids and a particularly fine example is that from the tomb of Kha, from Deir el-Medina, dating to the early part of the reign of Amenophis III. This is decorated with two duck heads, their bills made in yellow.

Animal and bird motifs were always popular in Egyptian art, and this is reflected in glass, particularly in the core-formed *Tilapia* (known as *bulti* in Arabic) fish vessels. They are usually decorated with coloured glass, but plainer examples also occur. These horizontal cosmetic vessels had stands when in use; the fish's mouth served as the rim.

Moulding and cold cutting

Since these two techniques are commonly used together on the same piece they are treated together here.

Mould-made vessels are found during the New Kingdom. The glass was either poured as liquid into a mould or heated as a powder. The British Museum has a fine kohl pot in blue glass with a gold rim which has a mould-made lid. The vessel body itself was probably moulded or cold-cut and the centre drilled out and pumiced smooth. Its date is not later than the time of Tuthmosis III. However, it is more commonly open forms (bowls and dishes) which are mould-made, though they are not very numerous in this period. They, too, may copy natural forms, such as the clam shell, more commonly made in faience or Egyptian blue.

In cold cutting, glass is worked as though it were a stone and is literally cut away. This is not a simple operation since, like other siliceous materials, it has a conchoidal fracture which is not conducive to cutting without the use of an abrasive wheel or saw. The crude shape of pieces to be cold-cut might be first cast in a mould, or a cast block of appropriate size could be provided. Quartz or flint implements were used to abrade the material using techniques already familiar to gem cutters.

Amongst the most skilfully produced pieces made in this way are two headrests made for Tutankhamun. One, in turquoise-blue glass, is made in two parts joined at the stem, the junction being

48. A turquoise-blue glass headrest of Tutankhamun. A skilful example of cold worked glass, it is made in two sections joined in the middle of the stem and with the join disguised by a gold band. Valley of the Kings. Eighteenth Dynasty. (Drawing by Kate M. Trott. Cairo Tutankhamun Exhibit Number 531.)

covered by an inscribed gold band (figure 48). The block shapes were probably first cast to the approximate shape in moulds. The other piece in darker blue glass has the upper part edged in gold foil. It, too, is inscribed for the king. A blue glass stand inscribed for Amenophis III is thought to have been worked from a cast block.

Glass sculpture in the round was always rare and difficult to produce. This must have been amongst the most highly prized classes of glass and frequently seems to have been produced under royal patronage. The Egyptians were the first people to use glass for sculpture.

The earliest pieces both belong to the reign of Amenophis II. The first is a small head of the king, now in the Corning Museum of Glass, New York. He wears a nemes headcloth and is made in now discoloured blue glass, probably moulded using the lost wax (cire perdue) process. The shape of the object required is first made in wax and then impressed into clay, a hole being left at a convenient place in the clay. The wax is then melted out, usually as the mould is fired, leaving a hollow of the desired shape. Into this is poured the molten glass. The mould is then broken away after cooling and annealing. It is therefore possible to use this type of mould only once.

The second piece is a shabti figure made for the king's steward Ken-amun, now in the Cairo Museum. This is in blue glass and has an inscription running down the centre of the body and five additional bands of inscription across it. The inscription was added after casting in a mould and details of the face and body were sharpened by carving at the same time. Only one other certain Eighteenth Dynasty glass shabti is known, also in the Cairo collection, dating to the reign of Tuthmosis IV. It was made for Heka-reshu, a tutor in the royal household, and is particularly fine. A third, poorer-quality, example, in a violet-blue glass, is inscribed for Men. It was made in a one-piece mould and so has a flat back. Though tentatively dated to the Nineteenth or Twentieth Dynasty, its true date and precise provenance are uncertain. It, too, is in the Cairo Museum.

No moulds for glass sculpture have survived (or have been recognised) but they must have been similar to those used for faience. A certain amount of detail would be included in the mould, but inscriptions, facial details and so on would be cold-cut and a substantial amount of reworking is often evident. The shabtis were almost certainly the products of royal workshops given as royal gifts to favoured officials.

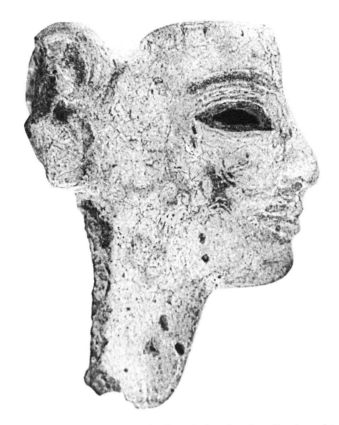

49. Glass inlay of a female face; originally red, the piece has discoloured to green. The eye is fully pierced, which is unusual. The eyebrow would have been inlaid. Provenance unknown. Late Eighteenth Dynasty. Height 36 mm. (Courtesy of the Petrie Museum of Egyptian Archaeology, University College London. UC 22077.)

Amongst the items from Tutankhamun's tomb, and now in Cairo, was a small figurine of the king, in a squatting position, made in blue glass. It is an extremely complicated shape, with one hand raised to the mouth and the other resting on the knee. On the back is a suspension loop. The piece would surely have been made by the lost wax technique. The figure was extensively reworked after removal from the mould.

Mention should be made of the blue glass inlays of the lappets of Tutankhamun's gold mask. Like a blue glass scarab of the king, they were probably moulded. The inlays, commonly used in the decoration of furniture or sometimes as architectural elements, were also made in moulds, of the one-piece, open type, since the back was required flat in any case (figure 49). These inlays are very common and occur in the full range of colours employed by the Egyptians, including clear glass, as found in the back of the Tutankhamun throne.

A different type of moulding is represented in the technique of *conglomerate* glass. This is sometimes called mosaic glass but the term is best reserved for true mosaic glass, which is not known from the New Kingdom. Conglomerate glass comprises coloured fragments melted together in a one- or two-piece mould until they fuse and produce an effect resembling ornamental stone. If made in a one-piece mould the interior surface would need extensive finishing after removal. The technique was most commonly used for open forms and is well known from Malkata.

10
The Third Intermediate and Late Periods

The decline in glass production

Until recently it seemed that glass making virtually died out after the Twenty-first Dynasty, not to be revived until the Twenty-sixth, but in the 1980s J. D. Cooney suggested that it may have lingered on, since a Twenty-sixth Dynasty shrine door of Amasis, and a similar piece of the Twenty-seventh Dynasty inscribed for Darius I, show exactly the same colouring as Eighteenth Dynasty glass. The colours include red, the secret of manufacture of which would have been hard to rediscover if once lost. It is suggested that this shows some continuity in glass making, albeit on a vastly reduced scale, throughout the troubled Third Intermediate Period. These two pieces represent the earliest dated late glass. Cooney has suggested that the decline in glass making may be the result of the increasing use of glassy faience at this time.

The best-known examples of this reduced output of glass are the vessels from the tomb of Nesikhons, a wife of a high priest of Amun who died during the reign of Siamun, a Pharaoh of the Twenty-first Dynasty.

Nonetheless, it is the Twenty-sixth Dynasty which marks the resumption of glass finds, though they are not plentiful until the Thirtieth (figure 50). At this time the industry seems to have been concentrated in Lower Egypt, between the Fayum and the Delta. Vessels were also widely imported, mostly from the eastern Mediterranean but also from Phoenicia.

Core forming

Core-formed vessels were being made throughout the eastern Mediterranean at this period and, as many were imported into Egypt, the recognition of native pieces is difficult.

Superficially, Late Period vessels resemble those of the New Kingdom (figure 51). They frequently have dark blue glass as a background colour and use coloured festoons as decoration. The glass itself, however, is rather different. Earlier glass vessels have generally suffered little as a result of burial, whereas these later pieces are often patchy or discoloured. The festoons are less well applied than in the New Kingdom and the trailed threads are often irregularly spaced and of differing widths, whereas the earlier pieces were more precisely executed. Earlier examples generally had the

50. Translucent blue palm bowl. Provenance unknown. Sixth or fifth century BC. 155.4 mm diameter. Decoration is believed to be wheel-cut. (Courtesy of the Pilkington Glass Museum. Object 1963/61.)

threads interrupted after every circuit of the body while on these later ones the threads wind around in spiral fashion. A second colour might also be added on top of the first. The threads are less carefully pulled or feathered, too, and festoons are generally confined to the middle of the vessel, with straight bands on other parts of the body. The colours also differ from their ancestors: orange replaces the earlier yellow and turquoise enjoys greater use than previously.

The shapes of late core-formed pieces are generally tall and slender, such as *alabastra, amphoriskoi* with button feet, *oinochoai* and *aryballoi*. These are the forms current in the Mediterranean world at this time rather than being purely Egyptian. Even vessels certainly made in Egypt form part of this Classical/Hellenistic tradition.

Moulding and cold cutting

At this period the *millefiori* ('thousand flowers') technique was developed. This involved the use of glass rods or canes, sometimes of several colours, which were fused together and drawn out, reducing the dimensions of the pattern. The canes were then cut to length and placed side by side in a mould. Depending on the pattern and the size of the canes, plain glass might be used to infill between the patterned sections. The whole assemblage was then heated until the canes fused together producing a colourful pattern of discs or

	ALABASTRA	AMPHORISKOI	ARYBALLOI	OINOCHOAI	HYDRIAI	UNGUENTARIA
VI–V CENT.					✗	✗
IV–III CENT.						✗
II–I CENT.			✗			

51. Chronological table of shapes of core-formed vessels of the Greek and Hellenistic periods, sixth to first centuries BC. (Courtesy of the Royal Archaeological Institute, after Harden in *The Archaeological Journal*, 125 [1968], figure 3.)

other shapes set against the background colour. The commonest pattern at this period was a relatively simple one of yellow circles or 'eyes' set against a green background. In principle the technique is like that of conglomerate glass.

Scarabs (figure 52) and other amulets continued. An amulet of Isis holding Horus, found at Matmar and now in the collection of

52. Scarab in blue glass. The piece is pierced for suspension. Unprovenanced. *c.*600 BC. Length 50 mm. (Courtesy of the Pilkington Glass Museum. Object 1967/10.)

the Fitzwilliam Museum, Cambridge, has been dated between the Twenty-second and Twenty-fifth Dynasties and is the only piece of glass sculpture before the beginning of the fourth century BC.

Mosaic glass

The earliest securely dated true mosaic glass belongs to the reign of Nectanebo II of the Thirtieth Dynasty, though it is possible that isolated pieces might be earlier. The mosaic is used on a shrine found at Abusir and is now in the Brooklyn Museum.

This technique reached its peak in Egypt and probably originated there. It required the production of glass rods or canes which were then fused together and drawn out. This retained the pattern whilst reducing it in scale so that delicate yet intricate designs could be produced in miniature. The earliest popular patterns were simple chequerboard schemes of black and white squares. The patterns were often backed with monochrome glass and might also be fitted into a mould to produce larger objects. The technique was generally used in the production of inlays for use in furniture or jewellery making.

11
The Graeco-Roman Period

Hellenisation of the glass industry

This period continues the traditions established during the Late Period, though the range of vessel forms and Mediterranean influences both increase as a result of the incorporation of Egypt into, first, the Macedonian/Ptolemaic Empire and then the Roman Empire.

The newly founded city of Alexandria soon became a thriving centre for glass production, developing its own specialised repertoire. Though core forming was common, there were also skilled blowers and moulders (*vitrearii*) and engravers (*diatretarii*).

Examination of a foundation plaque of Ptolemy III and Queen Berenice, in the British Museum, suggests that natron was used rather than plant ashes, though whether this represents a complete replacement of the earlier alkali source is not yet clear. Experiments were made in the colouring of glass, and several pieces are known which appear to be opaque black until held to the light, whereupon they appear a rich ruby red. Painted decoration was also applied to glass.

There is not space here to discuss Roman glass making in any depth, so only an outline of techniques and developments is given, though these were often used in combination.

Core forming

Core-formed vessels continued to be made during this period (figure 53) but were gradually replaced by blown vessels. Much of the finest Alexandrian work still employed this technique and Roman craftsmen used it to reproduce imitations of New Kingdom and Late Period pieces, though the result was often clumsy.

Moulding and cold cutting

Moulding glass and reworking by cold-cutting continued. *Millefiori* glass production was expanded, and Hellenistic bowls and dishes were quite widely produced.

A single piece of royal sculpture in the round is known, now in the Cairo Museum: the head of a king wearing the nemes head-dress. It is made in transparent wine-red glass to which opaque white glass in circular sections has been added to give an effect resembling imperial porphyry. The whole has been pumiced smooth

53. Core-formed amphora, in opaque white glass decorated in purple. The piece may have been made in the eastern Mediterranean, outside Egypt. Unprovenanced. Fourth to third century BC. Height 107.9 mm. (Courtesy of the Pilkington Glass Museum. Object 1963/47.)

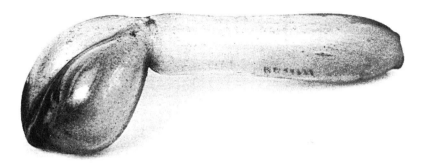

54. Phallus made in blown glass. From Hawara. Roman period. Length 100 mm. (Courtesy of the Petrie Museum of Egyptian Archaeology, University College London. UC 22498.)

after removal from the mould, and little detail is shown. Sculpture in glass remains rare.

The Alexandrian *diatretarii,* who produced cameo work, also produced glass faceted to resemble worked crystals and made the delicate openwork cage cups. One of these, found near Kabul in Afghanistan, is cut to show the Pharos lighthouse at Alexandria and was almost certainly made in the city.

Blown glass

At some time during the late first century BC glass blowing was discovered, probably somewhere on the Syrian coast, and the technique gradually spread to Egypt (figure 54). Molten glass is collected on the end of a hollow pipe. The glass maker then blows air into this mass (the *gather*) and, by swinging the mass on the end of the pipe and by rolling it on a flat surface or by blowing it into a mould, is able to shape the mass into a vessel. Pincers may also be used to assist in the shaping process. The technique allows even elaborate vessels to be produced more quickly and cheaply than by other techniques.

Glass blowing was slow to be adopted in Egypt but, once established, was practised with considerable skill and was often combined with cold cutting to produce cameo glass. In this technique, glass of one colour was blown and then dipped into glass of another, lighter colour. The two types of glass needed to be sufficiently similar for shrinkage to be equal, so that neither was cracked by the other. After cooling and annealing the outer glass would be delicately carved away, creating subtle changes of shade and colour and giving a sense of depth to the piece. This is the technique

55. Gold-thread *alabastron*. The piece is in black and white, brown and white, turquoise and gold leaf, set on dark blue. Part of the lip is missing. Possibly from Alexandria. Second to first century BC. Height 110 mm. (Courtesy of the Pilkington Glass Museum. Object 1974/19.)

56. Mosaic glass slice showing *ankh* and *was* symbols. It is in blue with the details in red, white, yellow and blue. Provenance unknown. First century BC to first century AD. Length 17 mm . (Courtesy of the Petrie Museum of Egyptian Archaeology, University College London. UC 22313.)

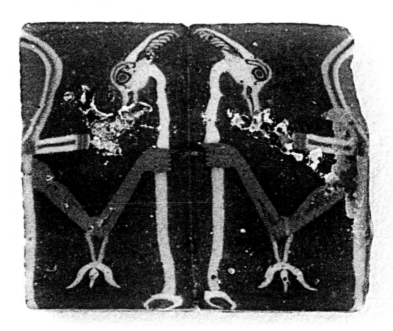

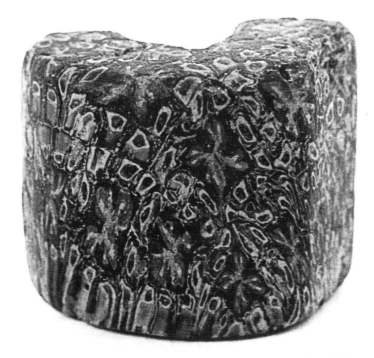

57. Millefiori/mosaic glass column drum or large cylinder bead. Dark blue ground with red, white and green flowers. Provenance unknown. First century AD. Diameter 35 mm. (Courtesy of the Petrie Museum of Egyptian Archaeology, University College London. UC 22066.)

employed on the famous Portland Vase in the British Museum, probably produced in Alexandria.

Gold glass

This was probably an Alexandrian speciality (figure 55). A gold sheet was placed between two pieces of glass which were then fused together at the edges. The most complicated piece known is a zodiac, now badly damaged, discovered at Tanis and now in the British Museum.

Mosaic glass

This technique reached its peak between the first century BC and the first century AD. Very intricate and complex patterns using numerous different colours of glass and irregular shapes were produced, including human and mythological figures and faces (figures 56 and 57). Where a face was to be seen frontally, only one half needed to be made; this could then be reduced to the desired size by stretching and then cutting sections from the rod. Since the sections were the same at each end, by placing two of them side by side a complete face could be produced.

The themes treated in mosaic glass are both Egyptian and classical, and it was commonly used in the production of decorative wall plaques and inlays.

As yet no workshops for the production of mosaic glass are known from Egypt, though evidence from a studio found at Gumaiyima near Tanis suggests that the craft may have been carried on by itinerant craftsmen.

By the early years of the first century AD Egyptian and Syrian glass makers were setting up new workshops in Rome itself and glass making — originally an eastern technology — spread rapidly throughout the Roman empire.

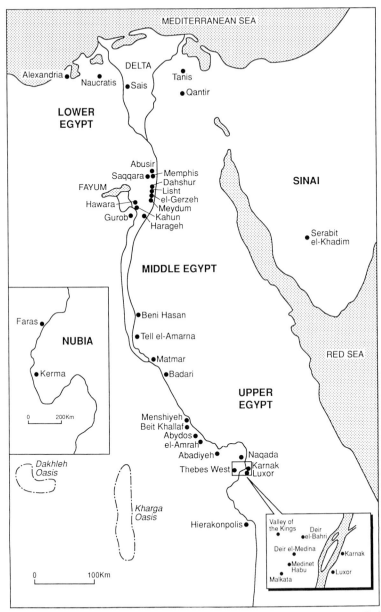

58. Map of Egypt showing main sites mentioned in the text. (Drawn by Robert Dizon.)

12

Glossary

Annealing: the process of slowly cooling a finished glass object to room temperature. This allows stresses in the glass to be released.

Batch: the mixture of soda, lime and silica, with any colouring agents, which produce glass when fused at high temperatures.

Bezel: that part of a finger ring which bears the design, or into which the stone is set (see also *shank*).

Cane: used here to mean a thin rod of glass. Cane and rod are sometimes used interchangeably.

Conglomerate glass: glass vessels made up from fragments of different coloured glass fused together in a mould. The fragments are usually angular. Since the pieces could, at least in theory, include pieces of cane or rod then the technique is a type of mosaic glass. (See *millefiori glass, mosaic glass.*)

Core: a shape, made in mud and/or dung, around which early glass vessels were formed. The friable core was removed on completion of the vessel.

Egyptian blue: calcium-copper tetrasilicate ($CuO\ CaO_4\ SiO_2$), a specific type of frit used as a pigment or sometimes in the making of objects or vessels. (See *frit*.)

Frit: the product of fritting. Frit may be ground for use as a pigment, used for the manufacture of objects, or melted for use in glass making. (See *fritting*.)

Fritting: the first stage in the making of ancient glass, involving a solid state reaction between quartz, lime and plant ash. The product of this process is frit. (See *frit*.)

Gather: also known as 'gob'. Literally the viscous molten glass gathered from the kiln on the end of a metal rod or blowpipe ready for working.

Lentoid: a shape reminiscent of a lentil. The term is commonly used when describing the vessel form also known as a pilgrim flask, namely a vessel circular in elevation but oval in plan.

Marver: a flat surface on which vessels are rolled during manufacture in order to make the surface smooth, assist in shaping, and sometimes to impress (marver-in) decoration.

Metal: a confusing and inaccurate term sometimes used to refer to the substance glass. Fabric is a more appropriate term.

Millefiori glass: used here to refer to glass vessels made from sections of glass canes fused together in a mould, for example the yellow eyes on a green ground found in the Late Period. Strictly it is a type of mosaic glass. The term, meaning 'thousand flowers', is strictly confined to floral patterns but is used here for cane designs other than the complicated mosaic designs of the first century BC to the first century AD. (See *conglomerate glass, mosaic glass.*)

Mosaic glass: used in different ways by different authors. It is used here to refer to figures and patterns made up from sections of glass rod. Examples are chequer-board patterns, human faces, hieroglyphs and so on. However, it could be used to refer to conglomerate and millefiori glass. (See *conglomerate glass, millefiori glass*).

Network former: an inorganic oxide which can be used to form vitreous materials. For ancient glass this is silicon dioxide (silica). However, silica has a melting point of 1710°C, far beyond the range of ancient glass makers, and so requires a network modifier to allow its use in glass making.

Network modifier: a substance added to the network former in order to enhance its working properties, usually to lower its melting temperature. For ancient glass, this is usually natron or plant ash. Alkali and silica together yield a glass which is water soluble, and to overcome this problem lime is usually added to the mixture.

Rod: used here to mean an elongated piece of glass which has been poured or pulled from a crucible and/or rolled to make a roughly cylindrical rod. Thin pieces are known as canes, though the two may be used interchangeably.

Seed: name given by glass makers to bubbles left in the glass where gases have not been able to escape before the mass solidified. In modern processes the temperatures are high enough to allow the gases to escape, but anciently this was a problem and, despite the use of fritting as a first stage in Egyptian glass making, some bubbles may still remain.

Shank: the ring part of a finger ring. This may not be a complete circle but rather a U-shape, the bezel closing the circle to make a complete ring. (See *bezel*.)

Skeuomorph: representation of one material or form in another, for example painted decoration resembling ropes or pottery shaped and textured as baskets.

Stones: lumps of unmelted raw material which, in modern glass making, settle out of the mass of molten glass during manufacture. Ancient Egyptian glass makers could not achieve sufficiently high temperatures for this settling process to take place and hence used a two-stage process, beginning with fritting.

13

Further reading

Bimson, M., and Freestone, I. C. 'Some Egyptian Glasses Dated by Royal Inscriptions', *Journal of Glass Studies*, 30 (1988), 11-15.

Boston Museum of Fine Arts. *Egypt's Golden Age: The Art of Living in the New Kingdom, 1558-1085 BC.* Museum of Fine Arts, Boston, 1982.

Boyce, A. 'Notes on the Manufacture and Use of Faience Rings at Amarna', in B. J. Kemp (editor), *Amarna Reports V*, Egypt Exploration Society, 1989, 160-8.

Cooney, J. D. 'Glass Sculpture in Ancient Egypt', *Journal of Glass Studies*, 2 (1960), 10-43.

Cooney, J. D. *Catalogue of Egyptian Antiquities in the British Museum IV: Glass.* London, British Museum, 1976.

Goldstein, S. M. *Pre-Roman and Early Roman Glass in the Corning Museum of Glass.* New York, Corning Museum of Glass, 1979.

Kaczmarczyk, A., and Hedges, R. E. M. *Ancient Egyptian Faience.* Warminster, Aris and Phillips, 1983.

Newton, R. G., and Davison, S. *Conservation of Glass.* London, Butterworth, 1989.

Noble, J. V. 'The Technique of Egyptian Faience', *American Journal of Archaeology*, 73 (1969), 435-9.

Nolte, B. 'Die Glasgefässe im Alten Ägypten', *Berlin, Münchner Ägyptologische Studien*, 14 (1968).

Riefstahl, E. *Ancient Egyptian Glass and Glazes in the Brooklyn Museum.* Brooklyn, Brooklyn Museum, 1968.

Tait, G. A. D. 'The Egyptian Relief Chalice' *Journal of Egyptian Archaeology*, 49 (1963), 93-139.

Tite, M. S. 'Egyptian Blue, Faience and Related Materials: Technological Investigations', in R. E. Jones and H. W. Catling (editors), *Science In Archaeology*. British School at Athens: Fitch Laboratory Occasional Paper 2 (1986), 39-41.

Tite, M. S., Freestone, I. C., and Bimson, M. 'Egyptian Faience: An Investigation of the Methods of Production', *Archaeometry*, 25, 1 (1983), 17-27.

Turner, W. E. S. 'Studies of Ancient Glass and Glass-Making Processes. Part I. Crucibles and Melting Temperatures Employed in Ancient Egypt at about 1370 BC', *Journal of the Society of Glass Technology*, 38, 183 (1954), 436-444T.

Vandiver, P., and Kingery, W. D. 'Egyptian Faience: the First High-Tech Ceramic', in W. D. Kingery (editor), *Ceramics and Civilisation 3*. American Ceramic Society, Columbus, Ohio (1987), 19-34.

Wulff, H. E., Wulff, H. S., and Koch, L. 'Egyptian Faience: a Possible Survival in Iran', *Archaeology* 21 (1968), 98-107.

14

Museums

Most museums with Egyptological collections include some artefacts of glass and faience in their displays. The following lists some of the more important collections. Intending visitors are advised to find out the times of opening before making a special journey.

United Kingdom
Ashmolean Museum of Art and Archaeology, Beaumont Street, Oxford OX1 2PH. Telephone: 0865 278000.
British Museum, Great Russell Street, London WC1B 3DG. Telephone: 071-636 1555.
Fitzwilliam Museum, Trumpington Street, Cambridge CB2 1RB. Telephone: 0223 332900.
Liverpool Museum, William Brown Street, Liverpool L3 8EN. Telephone: 051-207 0001.
Manchester Museum, University of Manchester, Oxford Road, Manchester M13 9PL. Telephone: 061-275 2634.
Petrie Museum of Egyptian Archaeology, University College London, Gower Street, London WC1E 6BT. Telephone: 071-387 7050, extension 2884.
Pilkington Glass Museum, Prescot Road, St Helens, Merseyside WA10 3TT. Telephone: 0744 28882.

Egypt
Egyptian Museum, Tahrir Square, Cairo.

France
Musée du Louvre, Palais du Louvre, 75003 Paris.

Germany
Ägyptisches Museum, Staatliche Museen, Bodestrasse 1-3, 102 Berlin.
Ägyptisches Museum, Staatliche Museen Preussischer Kulturbesitz, Schlossstrasse 70, 1000 Berlin 19.
Staatliche Sammlung Ägyptischer Kunst, Meiserstrasse 10, 8000 Munich 2.

Italy
Museo Egizio, Palazzo dell' Accademia delle Scienze, Via Accademia delle Scienze 6, Turin.

Netherlands
Rijksmuseum van Oudheden, Rapenburg 28, 2311 EW, Leiden.

United States of America
The Brooklyn Museum, 200 Eastern Parkway, Brooklyn, New York, NY 11238.
The Corning Museum of Glass, One Museum Way, Corning, New York, NY 14831.
Metropolitan Museum of Art, 5th Avenue at 82nd Street, New York, NY 10028.
Museum of Fine Arts, 465 Huntington Avenue, Boston, Massachusetts, 02115.

Index

Page numbers in italic refer to illustrations.